CONTENTS

Sonata no. 8, Op. 13 ("Pathétique")
C Minor
(1797?–8)

Attacca subito l' Allegro:

1) Short appoggiatura.

Adagio cantabile.

RONDO.
Allegro.

1) ![short trill figure]

2) Short appoggiatura.

Sonata no. 14, "quasi una fantasia"
Op. 27, No. 2 ("Moonlight")
C-sharp Minor
(1801)

Adagio sostenuto.

Si deve suonare tutto questo pezzo delicatissimamente e senza sordini.

sempre pianissimo e senza sordini

1) The pedal indications are Beethoven's.

Presto agitato.

30 • *Sonata no. 14, Op. 27/2 ("Moonlight")*

Bagatelle, Op. 33, No. 3

F Major

(1801–2)

Bagatelle, Op. 33, No. 7

A-flat Major

(1801–2)

Sonata no. 17, Op. 31, No. 2 *("Tempest")*

D Minor
(1802)

1) The fingering in italics and the pedal indications are Beethoven's.

1) Thus in the original edition; it
   can also be executed:

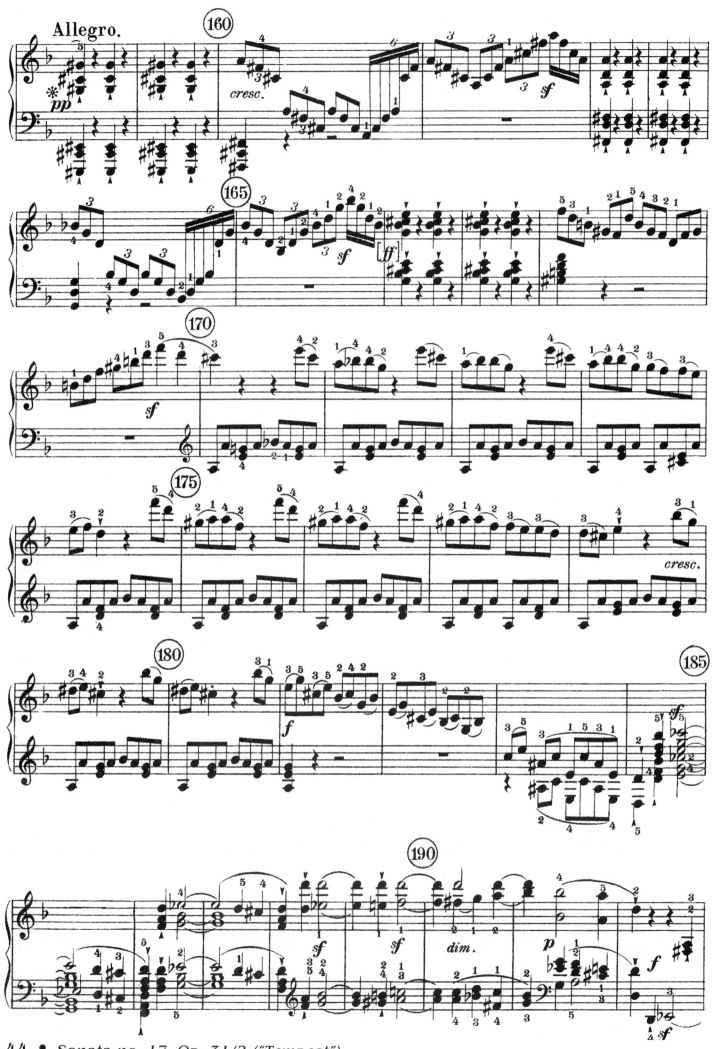

Allegro.

1) See the execution in m. 10.

Bagatelle, Op. 119, No. 5
C Minor
(1820–2, from earlier sketches)

Six Variations on an Original Theme, Op. 34

F Major

(1802)

VAR. I.

VAR.II. Allegro, ma non troppo.

VAR.III. Allegretto.

Fantasia, Op. 77

G Minor/B-flat Major

(1809)

Allegro ma non troppo.

Allegretto.

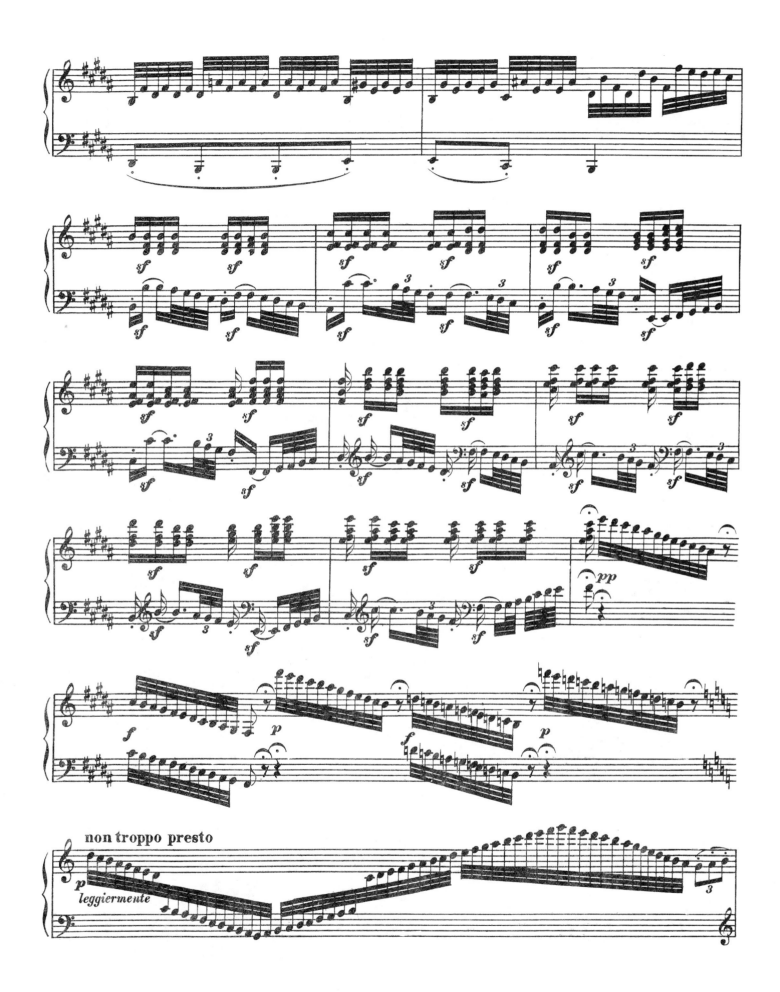

Minuet, WoO 10, No. 2

G Major

(1795?)

Six Bagatelles, Op. 126

(1823–4)

La seconda parte due volte.

Nº 2. Allegro.

Rondo a Capriccio, Op. 129
("Rage over a Lost Penny")
G Major
(1795)

98 • *Rondo a Capriccio, Op. 129 ("Rage over a Lost Penny")*

Andante, WoO 57 ("Andante favori")
F Major
(1803)

Andante grazioso con moto.

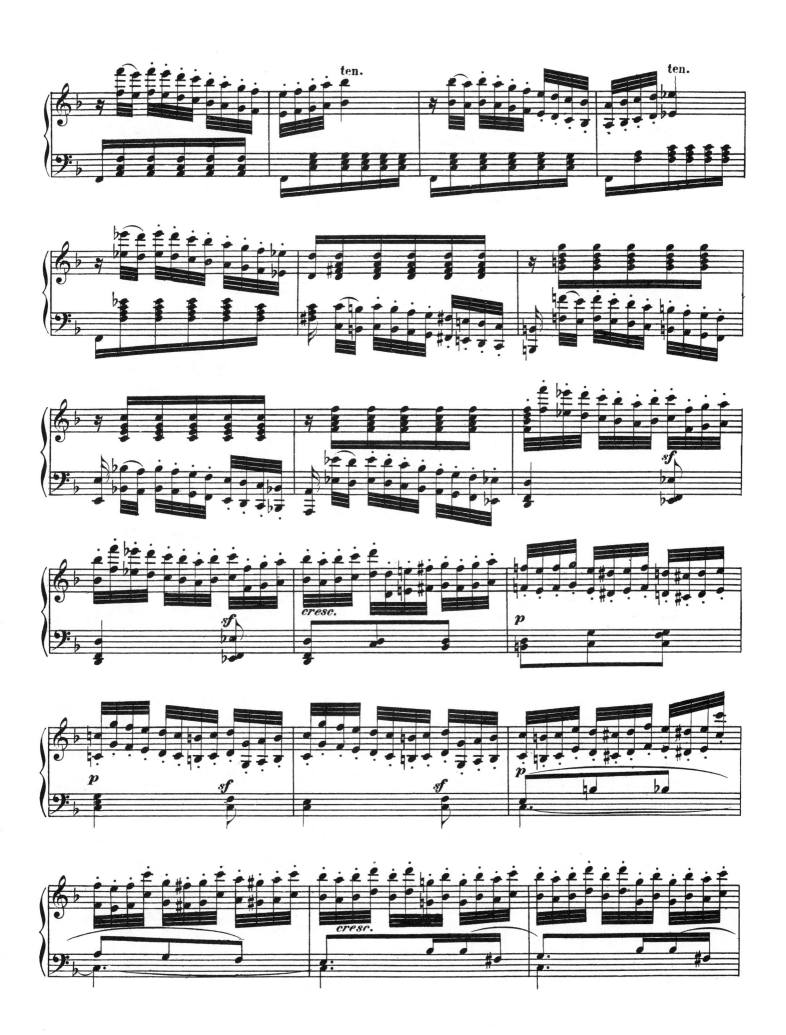

Bagatelle, WoO 59 ("Für Elise")

A Minor

(1808)

Minuet, WoO 82

E-flat Major

(before 1805)

Trio.

Mennetto da capo.

Sonatina, Anh. 5, No. 1
G Major
(1790–2?)

Moderato.

Romanze.

Sonatina, Anh. 5, No. 2

F Major

(1790–2?)

Allegro assai.

Seven Variations on "God Save the King," WoO 78

C Major

(1802–3)

Thirty-two Variations on an Original Theme, WoO 80

C Minor

(1806)

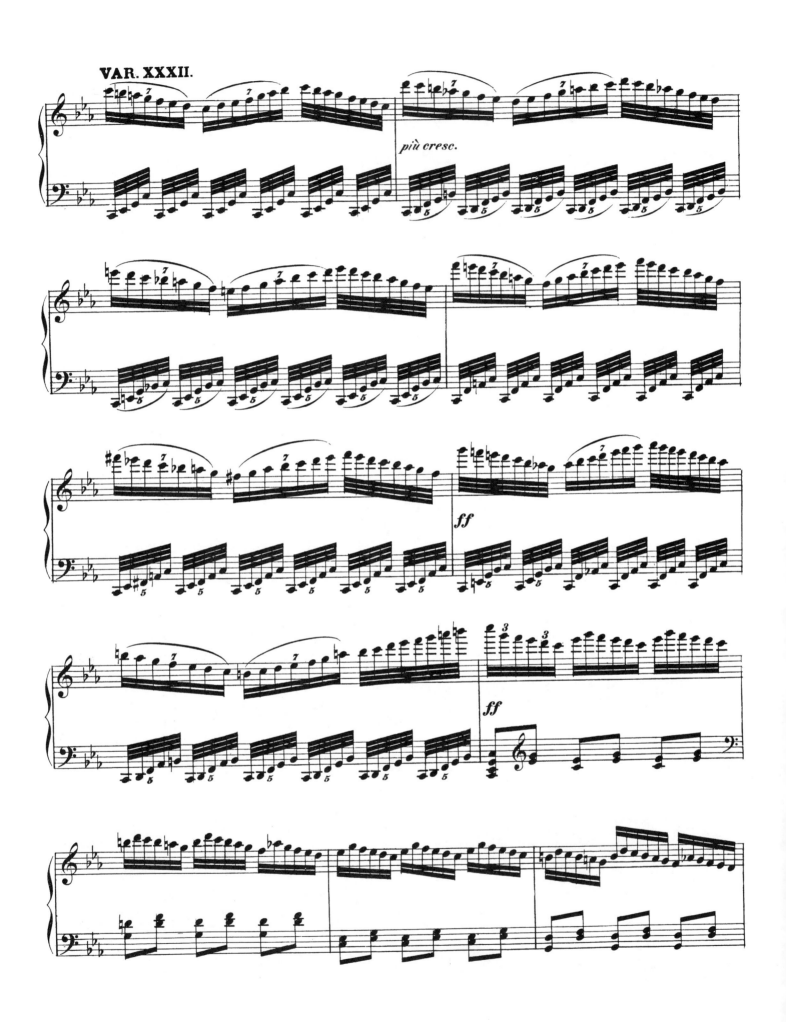

Seven Ländler, WoO 11

(1798?)

Sonatina, WoO 51

C Major

(1797?–8)

Adagio.